Me & My Dog

By Maxine Rock

Illustrated by
Amanda Haley

American Girl

For information, address:
Book Editor
Pleasant Company Publications
8400 Fairway Place
Middleton, WI 53562

Visit our Web site: **www.americangirl.com**

Printed in Hong Kong. Assembled in China.
01 02 03 04 05 06 07 08 C&C 10 9 8 7 6 5 4 3 2 1

American Girl Library® is a registered trademark of Pleasant Company.

Editorial Development: Elizabeth A. Chobanian, Michelle Watkins
Art Direction: Chris Lorette David
Design: Chris Lorette David, Camela Decaire
Book Production: Kendra Pulvermacher, Janette Sowinski
Illustrations: Amanda Haley

Library of Congress Cataloging-in-Publication Data

Rock, Maxine A., 1940-
Me and my dog / Maxine Rock
p. cm.
ISBN 1-58485-367-0
1. Dogs—Behavior—Miscellanea—Juvenile literature.
2. Dogs—Miscellanea—Juvenile literature.
[1. Dogs—Miscellanea. 2. Pets—Miscellanea.] I. Title

SF433 .R63 2001
636.7'0887—dc21   2001021008

Dear ^dog-loving American girl:

Imagine the **best** friend you could ever have. She's **kind.** She's there when you need a shoulder to cry on. And best of all: she likes you for *you.* Now, think about what makes your **dog** so special. Bet she's a lot like that best friend you just imagined!

Sure, your dog may sometimes feel like a big **responsibility.** But she will always love you and try to please you. In fact, a dog is probably the only friend who makes **your happiness** her biggest goal!

It's true—a dog is a girl's best friend. And you can thank her by being a good friend, too. This book will teach you how to keep your dog happy and have fun in the process. After all, treats might get her tail wagging, but your friendship is the greatest **reward!**

Your friends at American Girl

Puppy

Sure, you  love your dog. But what really makes her tick? The more you know, the better friend you'll be.

Love

Quiz! What Makes

Just how much do you know about dogs? Take this quiz to find out.

1. Because dogs are house pets, they don't have wild instincts.

 True   ☐ False

2. Dogs are able to think and interpret information.

☐ True   False

3. Dogs like their independence.

 True   ☐ False

Dogs Tick? Quiz!

4. Dogs like adventure and want every day to be different.

    ✓ True   ☐ False

My Neighborhood

5. A dog should feel like the least powerful member of your family.

    ☐ True   ✓ False

6. Dogs gather information about their environment by keeping an eye on everything.

    ✓ True   ☐ False

Answers

1. False

Your dog's ancestors were wild wolves. Over thousands of years, dogs have become domestic animals, meaning they live in human homes. But your dog still has the instincts her ancestors needed in the wilderness. Her behavior stems from these wild roots.

2. True

Dogs are smart creatures. Some psychologists believe a dog can understand up to 200 words or more—just like a two-year-old toddler. Dogs can also interpret tone and body language.

3. False

Your dog thinks of your family as her pack. Since wolves live in packs for hunting and security, your dog's wild instincts create the same need to be a part of a group. A dog needs regular interaction with you and your family to feel safe and happy.

4. False

Dogs like **routines**. Whether she's eating, exercising, or pooping, your dog prefers a schedule. Following a routine reassures your dog that her needs will be met.

5. True

To maintain order in your home, your dog must be at the **bottom** of your family's pack. The leader of the house should be a human! If your dog senses a lack of leadership, she might try to set her own house rules!

6. False

While some dogs have good vision, don't underestimate that wet nose! A dog relies on her nose to explore the world. In fact, a dog's sense of **smell** is 100 times stronger than a human's! Her nose is super sensitive, so be gentle.

A Dog's Life

You'll notice **differences** in your dog's **behavior** as she ages. Here's what to expect:

From Birth to Six Months

Your dog is a puppy, or a baby. Expect plenty of activity, because he'll want to explore everything. He might nip at you with his sharp baby teeth. He doesn't mean to hurt you; he's just playing. At this age, everything is a game.

Six Months to One Year

Your dog is like a teenager: fun, active, and a bit rowdy. If possible, take your "teen" to dog training classes. To avoid ending up with a litter of puppies, ask your parents about having your dog spayed or neutered. It can actually make your dog a lot happier and healthier.

One to Six Years

Your dog is fully mature. He is settling down and won't be quite as active as he was before. With your help and care, he will continue to be a healthy and fun-loving friend.

Six Years and Beyond

Your dog is still loyal and devoted, but now he may be slowing down. You may notice that he doesn't run as fast as he once did. However, a healthy dog can often maintain youthful vigor well beyond six years.

Old Age

Just like people, individual dogs appear to age differently. Many dogs stay active until they are very old, and proper veterinary care can keep them feeling good. Remember, old age is not a disease. Treat your dog with kindness, care, and respect.

What's Your Pooch's

Dogs have personalities, just like people do. Take this quiz to discover your dog's personality.

1. Ding-dong! The mailman's at the door with a package. Your dog . . .

   a. rushes to meet him, wagging her tail and eager to be petted.

   b. runs and hides behind the couch, peeking around to see what happens.

   c. runs to meet him, barking and growling forcefully with her hair raised.

2. Your dog is lying on the couch, a spot where she is not allowed. When you tell her to get off, she . . .

   a. jumps off immediately and comes running to you.

   b. jumps off and runs from your sight into another room.

   c. begins to growl, forcing you to remove her by pulling on her collar.

Personality?

3. You've just come home from school. Your dog greets you by . . .

   a. bounding up to you, wagging her tail and wanting to be petted.

   b. rolling over, showing you her belly, and sometimes peeing.

   c. being a nuisance, demanding attention by nudging and pawing at you.

4. While your dog is eating, you notice the water bowl next to her is almost empty. When you reach for the bowl, your dog . . .

   a. moves aside, allowing you to take the bowl away easily.

   b. lowers her body, cringing and looking up at you before she allows you to take the bowl.

   c. growls and barks at you, protecting the bowl and resisting your attempt to take it.

5. You and your friend are talking in your room. When your dog comes in, your friend reaches out to pet her. Your dog . . .

   a. goes right to her, tail wagging, and licks your friend's hand.

   b. hides behind you with her tail between her legs.

   c. growls and stares, with her ears, hair, and tail up.

Answers

If you answered . . .

Mostly **a**'s

Your dog is *Friendly*. She's easy-going, cooperative, and easily trainable. Friendly dogs thrive on attention, so the more time and affection you give her, the better. Whether you're teaching her a new command or simply taking her for a walk, your dog loves to be with you.

Mostly **b**'s

Your dog is FEARFUL. She wants to be at the bottom of your family's pack, because she needs a leader to feel safe. Talk to her softly and give her lots of encouragement. Make sure she has her own private spot. Don't tease her, and don't push her into situations that scare her. If she shows signs of fear, such as tucking her tail between her legs, be careful; she could bite. Gaining her trust is your main goal. Once she trusts you, enroll her in an obedience training class to help her feel more comfortable around others.

You aren't happy all the time. Your mood can change, depending on the situation. The same is true for your dog. The **key** to knowing your dog's personality is to watch her general behavior. How does she behave **most** of the time?

Mostly C's

Your dog is secure, but she's *Aggressive* and bossy. She wants to be the leader of your family's pack, so she might bite in an attempt to take control. When your friends come over, make sure your dog is in her kennel, or someone could get hurt. An obedience training class is a must.

BEWARE of DOG

Keys to Your

1 ♥ Walk. Stroll. Hike.

Dogs need exercise. Going out with you makes your dog's day, because she gets both companionship and a chance to explore.

2 ♥ Be gentle.

You wouldn't whap your friends with a rolled-up newspaper, would you? Never hit or yell at your pooch. Instead, give her lots of praise whenever she behaves well.

3 ♥ Feed her on time.

An empty stomach makes your dog unhappy. It can also make her nervous, grouchy . . . and sick. Healthy dogs eat on a schedule: same time, same place, same dish. Don't forget to keep her water bowl filled, too.

4 ♥ Give her a special spot.

You probably have a bedroom or a secret place where you can go to be alone. Does your dog? She should. Dogs need a hideaway that is snug, secure, safe . . . and special.

Dog's Heart

5. Don't let her run loose.

Keep your pet leashed on walks. Don't let her off the leash unless she is in an enclosed area or trained enough to come back on command.

6. Keep her looking great.

Brush your dog frequently with a dog brush, and give her baths regularly. Use special dog shampoo, and keep the water warm—not hot. When you're done, remember to put her collar and tags back on.

7. Spend time with your dog.

Your dog gets lonely without you. As her leader, she views you as the head of her "family," and if you ignore her, she assumes there's a problem. Give her as much attention as you can.

Wouldn't you like to know what your dog is trying to say when she **barks,** whines, h**o**wls, whimpers, or gggrowls? What does she mean when she jumps up, holds her tail down, or puts her ears back? Dogs can talk! You just have to know how to listen.

Dog Dictionary

Barking
"I'm listening for every sound, and I'm going to protect you."

High, shrill bark
"Something strange is going on, and it scares me."

Deep, growly bark
"I'm brave and protecting my home."

Barking that won't stop
"I'm bored and lonely. Come play with me!"

Yelping
"Ouch, ouch, ouch! Something hurts me!"

Whining
"I'm upset, and I need a hug."

Squealing
"Wow, am I happy!" or "I'm very pleasantly surprised."

Howling
"Oh, I'm so very, very lonely. I need you right away," or "I'm sick. Help me."

Dogs make a variety of noises. You should listen not only to the particular sound—a bark or a howl—but to the **pitch** and **depth** of the sound, too.

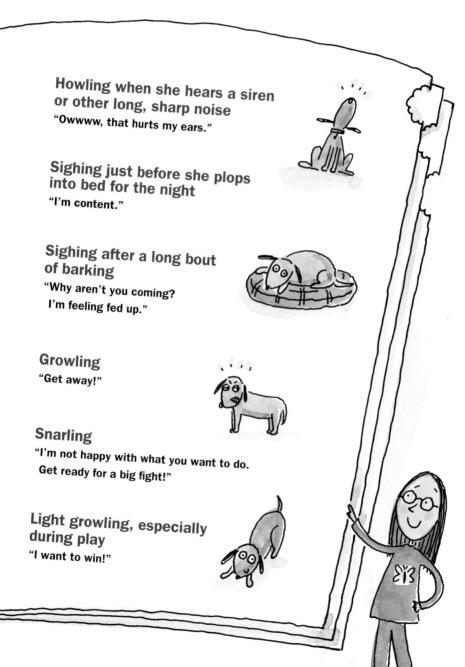

Howling when she hears a siren or other long, sharp noise
"Owwww, that hurts my ears."

Sighing just before she plops into bed for the night
"I'm content."

Sighing after a long bout of barking
"Why aren't you coming? I'm feeling fed up."

Growling
"Get away!"

Snarling
"I'm not happy with what you want to do. Get ready for a big fight!"

Light growling, especially during play
"I want to win!"

What Are YOU Saying?

When you say . . .   **Your dog thinks . . .**

Your dog does listen to you. But do you realize how your dog interprets your words and actions?

When you . . .   **Your dog thinks . . .**

Hug and pet her

I'm very special!

Play with her

She wants to have fun with me!

Never ever . . .   **Or she'll think . . .**

Ignore her   **or**   **Shout or speak harshly**

She hates me.

Ears and Tails Quiz

1. A wagging tail means your dog is just feeling good for no particular reason.

☐ **True**   ☑ **False**

2. Ears flat back against his head is your dog's way of saying, "I'm scared" or "I'm mad."

☑ **True**   ☐ **False**

3. If your dog is scratching his ears, it means he is confused and nervous.

☐ **True**   ☑ **False**

4. A tail hanging halfway means your dog is relaxed and feeling O.K.

☑ **True**   ☐ **False**

Dogs use body language to communicate. Your dog probably tells you the most with his ears and tail. Take this quiz to see if you know how to interpret your dog's **signals.**

5. When your dog's tail is between his legs, it means he doesn't feel well.

[√] **True** [ ] **False**

6. Your dog sticks his ears straight up when he's bored.

[ ] **True** [√] **False**

7. A tail held high means your dog is happy.

[ ] **True** [√] **False**

Answers

1. False

A **wagging** tail can mean he's happy, but only if it's combined with a reason for him to be happy, like seeing you. Some dogs wag their tails when they're in a defensive or challenging mood . . . so be alert and careful!

2. True

Ears **flat** against the head usually indicate some sort of distress or hostility. Some dogs do this while they're growling; they might bite!

3. False

A dog that is **scratching** his ears probably has fleas or an ear infection. If he keeps it up, tell an adult. Your dog may need to see a veterinarian.

4. True

A tail hanging **halfway** means, "I'm O.K." Your dog is relaxed and calm.

5. True

The lower the tail, the bigger the problem. If your dog's tail is between his legs, he is really scared, sick, or in trouble!

6. False

Pointing his ears straight up is your dog's way of asking, "What's going on?" He's curious, alert, and ready for action.

7. False

A tail held high is a threat. Your dog is saying, "Back off. I'm the boss." Watch for "flagging"—when the tail waves slowly back and forth. Unlike a wagging tail that is straight out, a flagging tail is high as a warning to watch out.

Don't rely on these signals alone! Your dog communicates by using his **whole** body. Even though his ears and tail send you signs, so do his fur, posture, and facial expression. Watching your dog's overall position is the key to understanding his body language.

Tough

Your dog  won't always be fun. Be prepared for some unpleasant surprises, like barking, breakage, and messes. Any good friendship takes time and energy. But a good friend like your dog is worth the trouble!

Training Tips

Let's face it: people appreciate a well-trained dog. But an untrained pet can often be a **pest.** Your dog will be happier and more welcomed by others if he is polite and **well behaved.**

Give **lots of praise**—such as petting, hugs, and a happy voice—whenever he does something right.

Your dog will learn **hand signals** more quickly than words. So when you say a command, use a hand signal at the same time.

Keep your cool. Never yell at your dog or hit him.

Have patience. It will often take several weeks before your dog masters a command.

You and your dog should **have fun** during training sessions. If you're not, take a break.

Don't train him for more than **20 minutes** at a time.

Consider enrolling your dog in an obedience class. Both of you can **learn from a professional.**

31

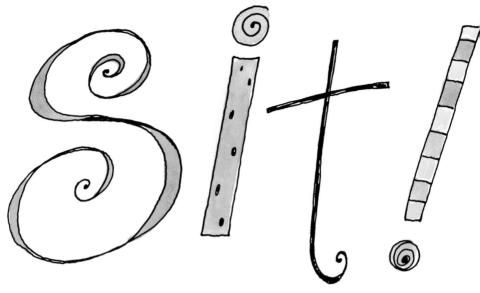

Sit!

1. Train her in a quiet place with nobody else around. And always use her leash.

2. *Gently* press down on her hind quarters, saying "sit," while pulling up on the leash. Always use "sit," not "sit down" or anything else. She needs to hear the same word every time.

3. When she sits, pet her and calmly praise her.

You probably can **teach** your dog to sit if she's over eight weeks old. It sounds easy, right? It's not. Your dog will wonder why she has to sit when she'd rather run around. **Be firm,** but have fun, too!

4. Instantly repeat the process. You want to make sure she can remember the lesson. When she performs well again, give her more praise and a treat. Pretty soon she'll sit by herself whenever you say "sit."

Tip: Have your dog sit whenever she gets attention, such as when you feed her, put her leash on, even pet her. She'll see you as the leader and appreciate the security.

Stay!

Teaching your dog "stay" is a little bit harder than "sit." What makes it hard is that you have to walk away from her to teach this **lesson,** and she will naturally want to follow.

1 ♥ Put your dog on a leash, and tell her to sit.

2 ♥ Put your hand out, palm down, close to her face and say "stay." Remember, use the exact same word each time.

3 ♥ Take one step away from her. If she moves, make her sit down again, and repeat the command.

4 ♥ Reward her right away when she finally stays put. Gradually lengthen the distance you walk away from her.

Star Pupil!!

Tip ♥

End your lessons on a positive note so your dog will feel good about the experience. Encourage her to do something she knows so you can reward her with lots of praise.

More Tips and Tricks

Tidy Up

My dog, Prince, is always chewing
my clothing. To fix this problem,
I ended up picking up after myself.
(What a concept!)

Callie, age 12, and Prince

Take Control

The biggest challenge is walking my dog.
She always runs! I shorten her leash and
then make it gradually longer as the
walk goes on. It works!

Autumn, age 12, and Savannah

Be Clever

Our poodle eats everything. To
solve this problem, we bought him
tons of bones, rag toys, and even
a postman doll!

Becky, age 12, and Max

Owning a dog isn't easy—for anyone. All dog owners have **problems** with their pets. Here are some solutions from girls like you.

Be Firm

I have a golden retriever who is always very hyper when you go into his pen. I realized that to keep him from jumping on me and getting me dirty, I just had to stand still and say firmly, "Meli, NO." It worked!

Kate, age 11, and Meli

Get Organized

I have a dog named Lucky. My toughest problems were feeding and walking her. My sister and I would always forget to do these things, so we made a chart.

Katerina, age 12, and Lucky

Have a Heart

My dog, Sierra, woke up in the middle of the night during thunderstorms. I would get up, take her to get some water, then calm her down by hugging her. She doesn't mind storms anymore.

Caitlin, age 11, and Sierra

Mix and Mingle

Rules of the House

Every pet must obey certain "house rules," such as no jumping onto the sofa. Tell your friends what the house rules are for your dog so that they don't accidentally help him get into trouble.

No Rough Play

It shouldn't be allowed. Not even a tiny bit. Your dog may become overexcited and bite. Tell your friends to always be gentle, to move slowly, and to not push, hit, or shout. Your canine protector will not think it's funny.

Collar and Leash

You know your dog must always wear his collar and tag and that he cannot be allowed to roam around the neighborhood. Do your friends know, too? For your dog's safety, make sure they do.

Your friends should know the basics about your dog's **training.** Tell them what to expect from your dog and what upsets or encourages him. In a way, you'll have to "train" your friends, not just your dog!

Don't Feed the Dog

You may want to remind your friends that sneaking snacks to the dog is not an act of kindness; he may get sick, become overweight, or get too full to eat the food that is good for him.

Privacy, Please

Your friends should know your dog's hideaway is off-limits. They must also be told not to touch the dog's dishes or toys. Your dog may not realize your friends are just curious. He'll want to defend his possessions and may threaten or even bite.

Quiz! The Canine

Solving the mystery of your dog's bad behavior may lead to you! Is YOUR behavior encouraging your dog to misbehave? Take this quiz to find out.

1. You're reading a good mystery book when your dog lets you know she needs to go outside. You ignore her and hope someone else will let her out.

a. Yes, that's me.
b. I might do this.
c. I'd never do this.

2. While you're eating breakfast, your dog begs for a bite. You sneak her a strip of bacon even though it's against the rules.

a. Yes, that's me.
b. I might do this.
c. I'd never do this.

Caper Quiz!

3. Your dog won't stop barking, and she's driving you crazy. Your first response is to yell "Shut up!" as loudly as you can.

a. Yes, that's me.
b. I might do this.
c. I'd never do this.

4. Your dog is not allowed on your bed, but you find her there— again. Getting her to obey this rule is too hard, so you give up and snuggle next to her.

a. Yes, that's me.
b. I might do this.
c. I'd never do this.

Mystery Solved!

If you answered a more than once . . .

You're the culprit!

Ignoring your dog and failing to enforce rules will encourage your dog to behave badly. Your dog will be a better student if you're a better teacher.

If you answered mostly b's . . .

You're no help.

You know the right way to handle situations, but you tend to take the easy route. Put a little more effort into caring for your dog, and you'll see results.

If you answered mostly c's . . .

You're innocent!

You are attentive to your dog's needs, and you give her the time and training that leads to good behavior. Keep up the good work!

Friends

Your dog will always have a special place in your heart. So use your imagination to show her you care. Whether you're (dreaming) up a new game or painting a picture of your pooch, the attention from you will keep her tail wagging.

Games for Two

High Hoops

Hold a hula hoop in one hand and a treat in the other. The hoop should be touching the floor. Lure your dog through the hoop with the treat. Say "jump!" as he goes through the hoop. After a few tries, raise the hoop a few inches off the floor. Reward your dog each time he makes it through the hoop. Practice jumping three or four times. Then give your dog a rest—and a big hug!

Hide and Seek

The next time you're playing fetch with your dog, run and hide while he's retrieving the ball. Call his name so he knows you're nearby. While he's looking for you, continue to call out to him. When he finds you, give him a treat, and try it again. The trick to this game is to be a good loser. It isn't any fun for your dog unless he gets to find you!

Dogs love **exercise** and **play,** especially when it means spending time with you. Yes, your dog will always be eager for a walk, but think of other things to do, too. Be creative!

Dog-stacle Course

Set up an obstacle course for your dog. Use a big cardboard box with open ends for a tunnel. Stack empty shoeboxes to make low hurdles. Use treats to lure your dog through the tunnel and over the hurdles. See how fast he can go!

Fetch and Squeak

The next time you're playing fetch, substitute a squeaky toy for the ball. Some dogs have natural hunting instincts, and chasing noise-making toys allows them to pretend they are hunters. Your dog will love chasing his squeaky "prey." (For your dog's safety, make sure the squeaker inside the toy isn't made of metal.)

SQUEEK!

Pet Projects

Beastly Bandannas

Well-dressed dogs will love these safe bandannas. Cut a bandanna in half diagonally. Fold the corners of the cut edge in a few inches toward the middle of the bandanna (figure A). Fold the cut edge down about 2 inches. Fold several more times. Make a few stitches on each side to hold all the layers together (figure B). Cut a 3-inch strip of self-stick Velcro tape and apply it to the ends of the bandanna. If the bandanna gets caught on anything, the Velcro will come loose, and your dog won't choke.

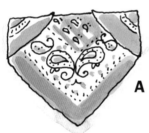

A

B

Starring Rover

Write an adventure and give your dog the starring role. What kind of trouble would she get into, and how would she get herself out? Use your imagination. If your dog could talk, how would her voice sound? What would she say? Would she have a favorite expression?

These unique crafts are fun ways to say "thanks" to your pooch for being such a good **friend.**

Canine Collage

Collect pictures of dogs that look like yours. Snip photos from magazines, save greeting cards, and add pics you've taken of your own dog. With glue or double-stick tape, create a collage on a piece of poster board. Use gel pens and markers to add captions and fancy borders.

Puppy Place Mat

Pamper your dog with a sweet pet place mat. Decorate a plastic place mat with permanent markers. Let dry. To clean a dirty mat, simply wipe it with a sponge.

Fridge Frame for Fido

Display a favorite photo of your dog in this magnetic frame. Glue craft sticks together to form a frame. Let dry. Paint Mod Podge (available at craft stores) on dog biscuits. Let dry. Glue to frame. Let dry. Center a photo of your dog. Use masking tape to attach it to the back of the frame. Stick 2 magnetic strips (buy in a roll at the craft store) on the top and bottom of the back of the frame. Make sure you display the frame out of reach of your dog, so she doesn't try to eat it.

Barking Up the Right T!

Put your pooch's mug on a T-shirt! Craft stores have computer transfer paper made especially for transferring photos to fabric. If you have a computer and scanner at home, scan the photo onto a sheet of transfer paper. If not, a printing shop can do this for you. Once the photo is scanned, place the paper face down on top of a plain white T-shirt. Have an adult iron over the paper, and voilá!

My Best Friend

My dog's name: Maggie

We picked this name because

Breed: Sheba Inu Chow mix.

Birthday: August nineth

Date my dog joined our family:

When I saw my dog for the first time, I thought She is so cute

(Paste a photo of you and your dog here.)

(Paste a photo of you and your dog here.)

Pick of the Litter

Date:

Place:

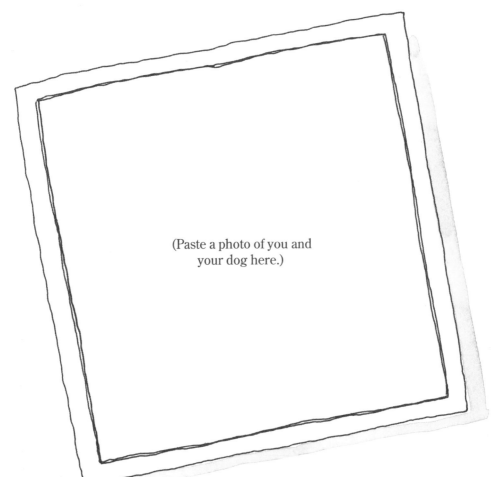

(Paste a photo of you and
your dog here.)

Photos of our first days together

(Paste a photo here.)

Date:

Place:

Date:

Place:

(Paste a photo here.)

Dog Dreams

At night, my dog sleeps _In her kennel_

Even though it's naughty, my dog would like

to sleep _with me_

While asleep, my dog will ....

....

....

I imagine my dog dreams about ....

....

....

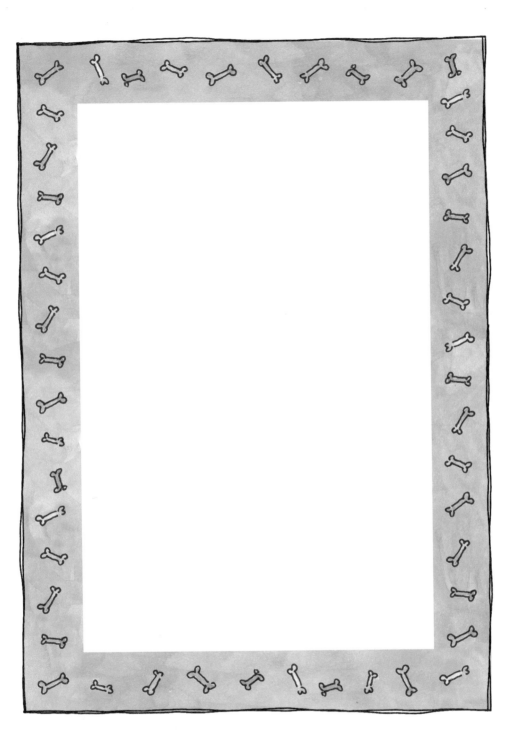

Here's a drawing of me and my dog.

(Paste a photo of you and your dog here.)

(Paste a photo of you and your dog here.)

Feelings

My dog is happiest when _we go to school_

 My dog is scared of _the cat_

When excited, my dog will _bark_

 I can tell when my dog feels guilty because

Food: _____

Toy: ~~Squirrel~~ Mickey

Game: fech

Trick: shake

Reward: cookie

Friend: Teddy

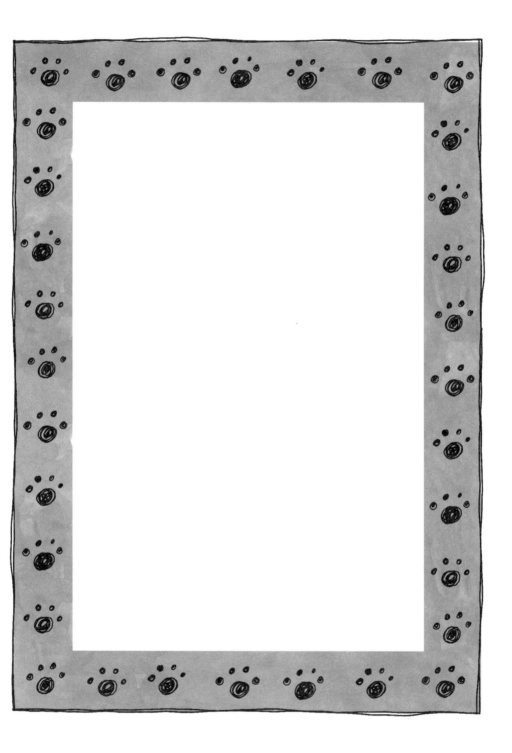

Here's a drawing of my dog and her favorite toy.

Memories

My favorite memory of my dog is ....

....

 The funniest thing my dog did was ....

....

The naughtiest thing my dog did was ....

....

My dog saved the day when ....

....

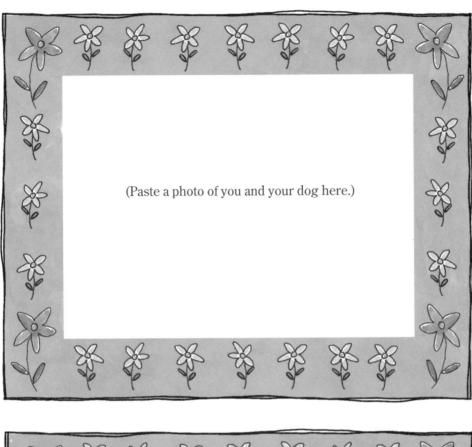

(Paste a photo of you and your dog here.)

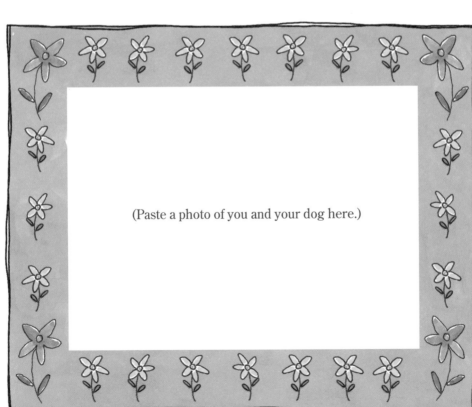

(Paste a photo of you and your dog here.)

Words my dog understands:

stay

sit

shake

go lay down

(Paste a photo here.)

(Paste a photo here.)

Heart to Heart

I love my dog because _She is nas I love here_

My dog's a good friend because _she dosn't bite_

I'm a good friend to my dog because _she is nice_

My favorite thing about my dog is _when she lays wit hime_

because _She is calm._

Free catalogue!

Welcome to a world that's all yours—because it's filled with the things girls love! Beautiful dolls that capture your heart. Books that send your imagination soaring. And games and pastimes that make being a girl great!

For your free American Girl® catalogue, return this postcard, call 1-800-845-0005, or visit our Web site at americangirl.com.

Send me a catalogue:

_____ / _____ / _____
girl's name   birth date

_____
address

_____
city   state   zip

_____
e-mail

(_____) _____
phone ❑ work ❑ home

_____
parent's signature   12583i

Send my friend a catalogue:

_____
name

_____
address

_____
city   state   zip

                                        12591i

Try it risk-free!

American Girl® magazine is especially for girls 8 and up. Send for your preview issue today! Mail this card to receive a risk-free preview issue and start your one-year subscription. For just $19.95, you'll receive 6 bimonthly issues in all! If you don't love it right away, just write "cancel" on the invoice and return it to us. The preview issue is yours to keep, free!

Send bill to: (please print)

_____
adult's name

_____
address

_____
city   state   zip

_____
adult's signature

Send magazine to: (please print)

_____ / _____ / _____
girl's name   birth date

_____
address

_____
city   state   zip

Guarantee: You may cancel at any time for a full refund. Allow 4–6 weeks for first issue. Non-U.S. subscriptions $24 U.S., prepaid only.
© 2001 Pleasant Company   K14L6